**Removed from
library collection**

D0847788

J 932 H

Horrible jobs in

ancient Egypt /

Plymouth District Library
223 S. Main St.
Plymouth, MI 48170

Aug 2014

J 932
H

HORRIBLE JOBS IN

ANCIENT EGYPT

Gareth Stevens
Publishing

ROBYN
HARDYMAN

Please visit our website, www.garethstevens.com.
For a free color catalog of all our high-quality books,
call toll free 1-800-542-2595 or fax 1-877-542-2596.

Library of Congress Cataloging-in-Publication Data

Hardyman, Robyn.
Horrible jobs in ancient Egypt / by Robyn Hardyman.
    p. cm. — (History's most horrible jobs)
Includes index.
ISBN 978-1-4824-0325-1 (pbk.)
ISBN 978-1-4824-0327-5 (6-pack)
ISBN 978-1-4824-0324-4 (library binding)
1. Occupations — Egypt — Juvenile literature. 2. Job descriptions — Egypt —
Juvenile literature. 3. Egypt — Civilization — To 332 B.C. — Juvenile literature. I.
Hardyman, Robyn. II. Title.
HF5382.5.E3 H37 2014
932—dc23

First Edition

Published in 2014 by
Gareth Stevens Publishing
111 East 14th Street, Suite 349
New York, NY 10003

© 2014 Gareth Stevens Publishing

Produced by Calcium, www.calciumcreative.co.uk
Designed by Simon Borrough
Edited by Sarah Eason and Rachel Blount

Cover Illustration by Jim Mitchell

Photo credits: Dreamstime: Alanesspe 45, Basphoto 10, 12, 23, 41,
Charlesoutcalt 34, Danbreckwoldt 15t, Dphotos 19, Eishier 38, Eleaner 30,
Foto280 21, Heywoody 6, 16, Jiawangkun 7, Linutes7 40, Mik122 17,
Neilneil 37, Prehor 42, Ralukatudor 28, V0v 36, Wrangel 5, Xiehangxing 22;
Shutterstock: Bestimagesevercom 24, Bzzuspajk 33, Farres 35, Jsp 27, Oleg Kozlov
31, Netfalls / Remy Musser 39, Elzbieta Sekowska 11, Przemyslaw Skibinski 44,
Jose Ignacio Soto 4, WitR 14; University of South Florida: Clip Art ETC 15b, 18b,
20, 32r; Wikipedia: 8, CaptMondo 18t, Dmitry Denisenkov 25, Keith Schengili-
Roberts 32l, Shawnlipowski 9, Neithsabes 43, The Yorck Project 26, 29.

All rights reserved. No part of this book may be reproduced in any form without
permission from the publisher, except by reviewer.

Printed in the United States of America.

CPSIA compliance information: Batch #CW14GS: For further information contact Gareth Stevens, New York, New York at 1-800-542-2595.

Contents

Chapter One Ancient Egypt 4

Serving the Pharaoh 6

Servant of Queen Merneith 8

Chief Bleacher 10

Gory Embalmer 12

Chapter Two Working on the Pyramids 14

Quarry Worker 16

Stone by Stone 18

Chiseling and Sharpening 20

Paint Mixer 22

Chapter Three Egyptian Life 24

Lowly Farmer 26

Busy Housewife 28

Canal Digger 30

Brick Maker 32

Reed Cutter 34

Barber and Wig Maker 36

Coffin Maker 38

Chapter Four Away from Home 40

Miserable Mining 42

The End of the Pharaohs 44

Glossary 46

For More Information 47

Index 48

Chapter One
Ancient Egypt

The ancient Egyptians developed an advanced civilization that flourished about 5,000 years ago. It lasted for almost 3,000 years, and some things from that time have survived for thousands of years more, to the present day. They tell us a lot about the lives of ancient Egyptians.

An Ordered Society

Society in ancient Egypt had distinct levels, and everyone had to know their place. At the top was the ruler, called the pharaoh. He was very powerful. Below him were the priests and officials, who ran the religious temples and the government. Then came the mass of the people—the workmen, farmers, and craftsmen. At the bottom were the poor slaves. These were the people who did the most miserable jobs.

Impressive monuments from ancient Egypt, such as these ram-headed sphinxes from the Temple at Karnak, near Luxor, are still standing today.

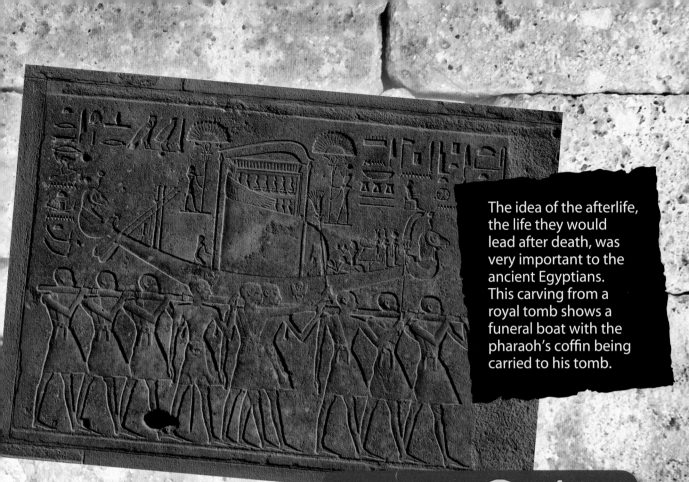

The idea of the afterlife, the life they would lead after death, was very important to the ancient Egyptians. This carving from a royal tomb shows a funeral boat with the pharaoh's coffin being carried to his tomb.

Working to Survive

For some miserable workers, their jobs were not even paid. They were simply part of everyday life. They were tasks that had to be done just to survive. Work was done every day, apart from a few holy days of the year, when people went to the temple. People made many of the things they needed, such as pots for cooking and storing food. Other goods were exchanged, or bartered.

A Life-Giving River

Life in Egypt depended on the Nile River. It provided water for farming, fish for food, and transport for travel and trade. When it flooded every year in summer, it dumped fertile mud onto the surrounding fields. This meant that crops could be grown in them, to feed the people. Without the precious water from the river, everyone would starve because the rest of the land was dusty and dry.

Serving the Pharaoh

The pharaoh was the most powerful man in the land. In theory the whole country belonged to him, so he could hand out land and favors to people—or make their lives a misery—as he wished. In general, however, the pharaohs were good rulers, who made their country great.

Hosts of Helpers

An army of helpers served the pharaoh. Some had powerful jobs and a comfortable life. The governors of each province, and the tax collectors, had a pretty good life and ran the country well. The pharaoh rewarded them with amazing gifts. There were other jobs for the pharaoh that were much less pleasant.

Pharaohs had lots of servants to cater to their every need.

A Female Pharaoh

The first female pharaoh was Hatshepsut, in 1518 BC. She became ruler when her husband died, and her son was too young to rule. She was a very successful ruler, too. She encouraged trade and prosperity, instead of going to war with Egypt's neighbors. After 20 years, though, her son rose up against her and seized power for himself.

At the temple Hatshepsut had built for herself, there were at least 10 of these large kneeling statues of her. She is holding offerings to the god Amun.

Bodily Needs

At home, servants provided for all the pharaoh's needs. These jobs were risky—displease the pharaoh, and you would certainly pay. Barbers shaved him and cut his hair. Hairdressers looked after his wigs. One servant bathed him in scented oils, another even cut his toenails! Would you like having the job of Bearer of the Royal Sandals? One pharaoh, Pepi II, apparently smeared his servants with honey, to keep the flies away from himself in the hot Egyptian sun.

Servant of Queen Merneith

Queen Merneith was a ruler in the very early history of Egypt, in about 2970 BC. She wasn't a pharaoh but ruled until her son Den was old enough to take over.

These servants are dancing for their mistress at a feast.

Life Is Hard ...

Being Merneith's servant was hard work. Her servants were responsible for her clothes and for looking after her hair. To dye her hair the servants used cows' blood, snake fat, and ravens' eggs—yuck! When a servant's mistress died, their job got much worse.

... And Then You Die

Ancient Egyptians believed in life after death. They preserved a person's body so that their spirits, *ka* and *ba*, could continue to use it. In the afterlife you continued with all the activities you had enjoyed on Earth. You kept the same status, too. For a queen to do all this in comfort and style she needed lots of objects to be buried with her—and servants!

When Merneith died, her tomb was surrounded by many smaller burials—servants who were sacrificed and buried alongside her so they could attend to her in the afterlife. They were probably poisoned or strangled—not much thanks for a life of service.

Shabtis Save Lives

All these shabti figures were buried in tombs, to serve the dead in the afterlife.

Luckily the brutal practice of sacrificing servants was stopped after a while. Instead of killing servants, small statues were made of them, called *shabtis*. These were placed in the tomb, to look after the royal person in the afterlife.

Chief Bleacher

It was the job of the chief bleacher to keep the royal clothing bright white. They had to get it right, or the pharaoh would show his displeasure.

The pharaoh on the right of this painting has pleats in his kilt.

A Royal Wardrobe

Pharaohs had lots of clothes, for every occasion and every part of their body—tunics, kilts, aprons, shirts, socks, scarves, caps, gloves, and headdresses. Their underwear was a triangular loincloth. The fanciest kilts had lots of small, stiff pleats. It must have been a tough job to make them all.

The waters of the Nile River were used for doing the laundry, but they also held hidden dangers!

Wash Day

Laundry was taken down to the banks of the Nile. It was scrubbed hard in river water with a detergent made using castor oil and lime. To get clothes really white the chief bleacher used natron. This was a type of salt, the same substance used to make mummies of dead bodies. To make parts of the clothes stiff, starch was used. The clothes were rinsed, wrung out, and put out to dry in the hot sun. There was an unusual hazard in this process—the river was full of crocodiles! If the laundry workers escaped the crocodiles, they still might have caught the horrible parasites and worms that lived in the river. They carried awful diseases that made people very sick.

Egyptian Fashion

Clothes were expensive, and the poorest people wore very little. Pleating in clothes was a sign of status, because it took a lot of work. The pharaoh might add a leopard skin to his outfit, slung over his shoulder to show his wealth.

Gory Embalmer

The ancient Egyptians believed you needed your body in the afterlife. If you were important, like the pharaoh, your body was preserved. This grisly task was the job of the embalmer.

A Home for the Spirits

Your body after your death was the home of your spirits, *ka* and *ba*. To keep the body from decaying, all the soft parts inside were removed. The embalmer removed the brain by pushing a hook up the nose and pulling. He then made a cut on the body using a "ripper" so that he could remove the internal organs, apart from the heart. This was left behind because it contained the person's soul. Each organ was put in a special canopic jar. These were placed in the tomb because the person would need them in the afterlife.

Anubis was the Egyptian god of mummification. He is always shown with the head of a jackal.

Stuffing and Wrapping

Next the embalmer packed the body with natron salts, and left it to dry for 40 days. Then he filled it with dry sawdust and fragrant herbs. He carefully wrapped it in layers of linen bandages. Now it was a mummy. The final stage was the "Opening of the Mouth" ritual. This meant the dead person could eat and drink in the afterlife. Offerings, some liquid, were made. A slit in the outer bandages of the mummy was sometimes made over the mouth. The embalmer's horrible job was done, and the body was ready for the coffin.

The embalmer would use hooks and a "ripper" to cut and pull out the internal organs of dead people.

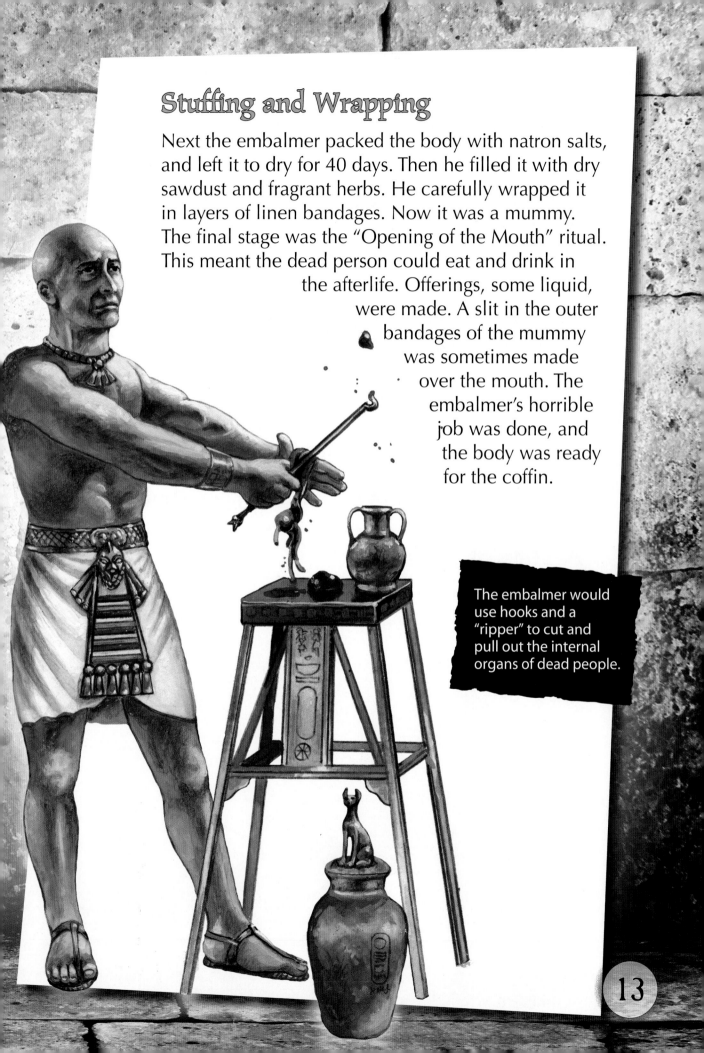

Chapter Two
Working On the Pyramids

The pyramids at Giza, in Egypt, are one of the wonders of the ancient world. These tombs of the pharaohs rise out of the desert like shining monuments. They weren't the first pyramids to be built, but their creation certainly took years of backbreaking work by thousands of poor laborers.

A Time of Tombs

Early Egyptian pharaohs were buried in underground chambers below rectangular buildings. The first pyramid was built for pharaoh Djoser in 2650 BC. Its stepped sides made a stairway to the sky so Djoser could reach the sun-god, Amun-Ra. The Great Pyramid at Giza was built for pharaoh Khufu in 2589 BC. Later pharaohs were not buried in pyramids because tomb robbers began to steal their treasures.

The large pyramid in the middle was for Khufu. The two on either side were for his successors Khafre and Menkaure. The small ones in front were for the pharaohs' wives.

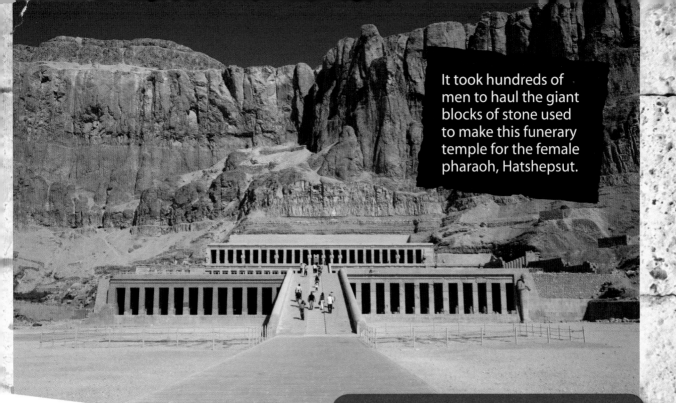

It took hundreds of men to haul the giant blocks of stone used to make this funerary temple for the female pharaoh, Hatshepsut.

Skill and Hard Labor

It took great skill to design a royal tomb pyramid. As soon as he took power, the pharaoh would demand that work started on his tomb. He wanted the very best, from the most talented workers around. He ordered huge teams of architects and builders to plan his journey to the afterlife. The pyramids were only one part of the plan. There was a temple, for making offerings, and a long causeway to the place where the body would rest after its journey down the Nile. Thousands of ordinary Egyptians put these grand plans into effect. They worked long hours every day, in the boiling hot sun. They respected their pharaoh, but they must often have longed for a rest from their horrible jobs.

The Setting Sun

All royal tombs were built on the west bank of the Nile. This was the side where the sun set, and so the pharaoh could join the sun-god in the afterlife.

Quarry workers, stone masons, and laborers worked very long hours to build the pyramids.

Quarry Worker

The Great Pyramid at Giza was built using about 2.3 million blocks of limestone! Each one of these weighed at least 2.7 tons (2.5 mt). It took about 20,000 to 30,000 workers about 20 years to complete, and it was absolutely backbreaking work.

Out of the Ground

Stone used to build pyramids was dug from quarries on the bank of the Nile. Quarry workers had the miserable job of splitting giant blocks of limestone away from the surrounding rock, using wooden wedges. These were soaked in water so that they expanded, breaking the rock. Most of the time the quarry workers worked underground in near darkness. The vast blocks were rolled away on tree trunks, onto huge sledges. Teams of men pulled these sledges to the barges that carried them across the river to the pyramid site.

An overseer would shout at the quarry workers to hurry them along if they were working slowly. They were sometimes whipped, too.

Yet More Stone

As well as limestone and granite, workers had to quarry other stones for the project. These included marble and alabaster, for making statues and floors, and basalt for making the coffin, which was called a sarcophagus.

Even Tougher Granite

If quarrying limestone was tough, quarrying granite was even worse because it's incredibly hard. Red and black granite were quarried at Aswan, in the south of Egypt. This stone was used for decorating the tomb. Laborers worked outside in the scorching sun, banging away at the granite using the pointed end of an even harder stone.

This obelisk is made from granite. Quarrying granite was a truly horrible job.

17

Stone by Stone

Once the stone blocks reached the building site, they had to be dragged to the pyramid and raised into position. The huge blocks were dragged by the quarry workers on wooden sledges along paths they had made of timber. No wonder it took 20 years!

The stone blocks used to build pyramids were huge and could be moved only on wooden sledges.

An Army of Workers

The skilled jobs were done by full-time workers, but most of the laborers on the project were farmers. When the Nile flooded every year, they left their fields and went to work on the pyramids, instead of paying taxes. The workers lived in cramped, smelly huts. Their work was exhausting and sometimes dangerous. They weren't even paid in money, but in grain, oil, or cloth.

Farmers left their fields to help build the pyramids when the river flooded the land.

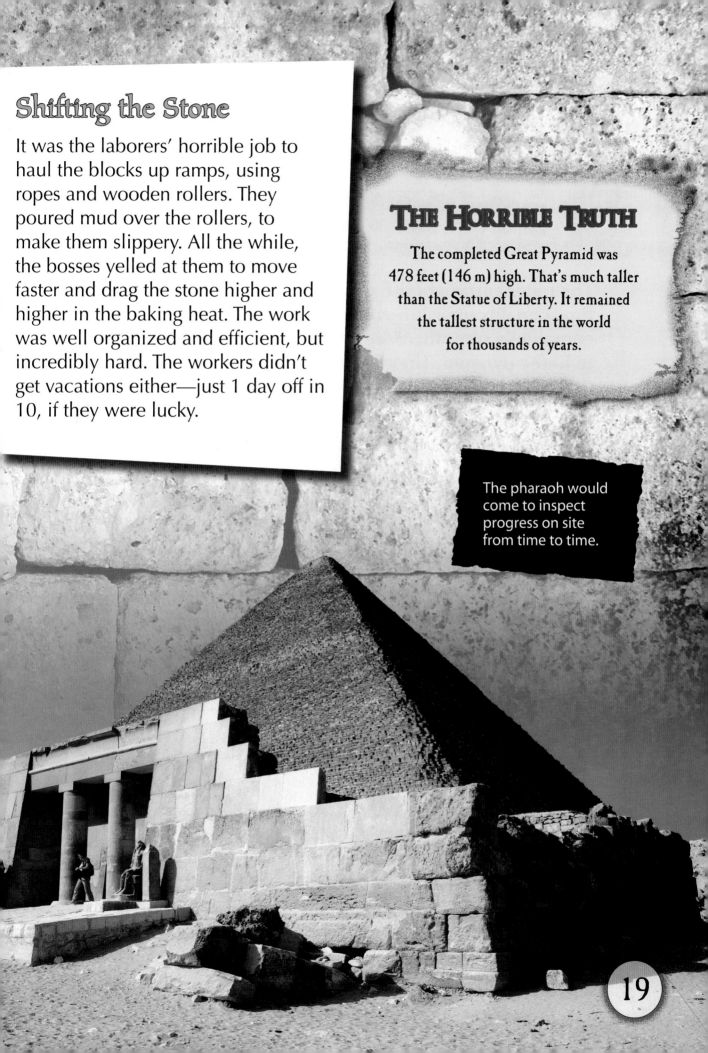

Shifting the Stone

It was the laborers' horrible job to haul the blocks up ramps, using ropes and wooden rollers. They poured mud over the rollers, to make them slippery. All the while, the bosses yelled at them to move faster and drag the stone higher and higher in the baking heat. The work was well organized and efficient, but incredibly hard. The workers didn't get vacations either—just 1 day off in 10, if they were lucky.

THE HORRIBLE TRUTH

The completed Great Pyramid was 478 feet (146 m) high. That's much taller than the Statue of Liberty. It remained the tallest structure in the world for thousands of years.

The pharaoh would come to inspect progress on site from time to time.

Chiseling and Sharpening

The outer surface of the pyramid was faced with the finest quality limestone blocks, laid together to make it completely smooth. More laborers had to shape these, to fit the pyramid. They had only simple tools to do this, and they needed lowly support staff to help them.

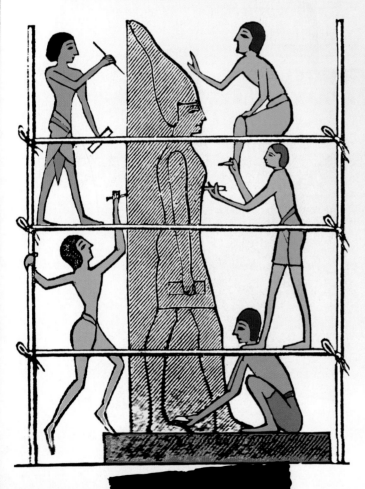

Stone masons worked in searing heat and for many hours at a time.

Skilled but Scary

Stone masons chiseled the huge blocks of limestone and were skilled at what they did. They had to chip away at each block, to make it fit perfectly. They did this with chisels made of copper, the hardest metal then known. Hour after hour, they banged away at the chisel with a wooden mallet. And they had to be quick. All the time, more and more blocks were lined up to be put in place. Sweaty hands, slipping chisels, and flying stone fragments meant the masons often suffered injuries. Their chisels quickly got blunt.

Sharpening at Speed

It was the job of the chisel sharpener to work with the stone masons. All day long they took the blunted chisels, sharpened them, and gave them back. In the heat of the day, under pressure to be quick, it was miserable work.

Topping It Off

The last block to be positioned was the pointed capstone, a mini-pyramid itself. Putting this in place accurately was a delicate operation because there was little room at the top of the pyramid! Finally, the job was done. The ramp was slowly demolished, from the top down. As the weary workers descended the pyramid, they polished the outside surfaces with rounded stones, to make them gleam.

The completed pyramid would have gleamed in the hot sun.

Paint Mixer

Deep inside the pyramid, more men labored on the pharaoh's tomb chamber itself. One of the most skilled jobs was that of tomb painters. They painted scenes and inscriptions to help the pharaoh in the afterlife. They were supported by more poor laborers, who prepared the surfaces and the paints.

Figures were shown with their head and feet in profile, and their body with a front view.

A Daily Grind

Once the chambers had been cut out of the rock, the walls were smoothed and plastered. A grid was drawn on the wall, to make sure the design of the painting was right. Then the images were outlined in red ink, before being filled in with paint. The paints were mostly black, blue, green, yellow, red, and white. These were made from local minerals, ground into a powder and mixed with egg white or tree resin, to make them sticky. It was the lowly job of the paint mixer to mix these paints all day long. Deep underground, they worked in very dim light, with only oil lamps to guide them.

This painting from the temple at Karnak shows the relief painting technique.

What a Relief

After the Pyramids

Even after pharaohs stopped building pyramids, there was still plenty of work for paint mixers. The huge temple complexes they built, for example at Karnak, were covered with painted decorations. At least now the paint mixers were working outdoors in the daylight!

Some scenes were painted in relief. This meant that the background was cut away, leaving the figures and other important features standing out from the surface. The background was painted with inscriptions and other details.

Chapter Three
Egyptian Life

More than 90 percent of the land of Egypt was desert. People lived and worked on the other 10 percent, the area made fertile by the Nile River. There were many good things to enjoy in their lives, but also hardships and dangers.

Good Times and Bad

Egypt was a wealthy country. The land usually produced enough food for most people, so they did have some leisure time. People enjoyed music, dancing, feasting, and partying. Life also had its perils, however. There were plenty of dangerous creatures around. Snakes and scorpions inflicted harmful bites that could even be fatal. The Nile River, although a source of life, could be deadly if crocodiles attacked people.

Horus was the falcon-headed god. He was one of the most important ancient Egyptian gods, and the son of the god Osiris and goddess Isis.

Religion

Religion was an important part of daily life. The gods looked after the people, and so the gods had to be looked after, too. Temples were built as homes to the gods, and people left offerings for them. Most people wore an amulet, a magical charm, to protect them from harm. This even went with the dead into their tomb.

Senet

A popular pastime was to play a board game called senet. The aim of the game was to reach the kingdom of the god Osiris. On the checkered board were images of helpful or harmful things you could land on, on the way there.

Four senet boards were found in the tomb of the pharaoh Tutankhamun. This is one of them.

Lowly Farmer

Most people in ancient Egypt lived off the land. Peasant farmers depended on the flooding cycle of the Nile, which made the soil fertile enough to grow crops. It was a tough routine.

This farmer is plowing his fields with a team of oxen.

The Farming Year

The waters of the Nile recede in October. That is when farmers sowed their seeds and looked after their crops of barley or emmer, a type of wheat. Harvest time was between February and June, before the river flooded again in July.

Paying Taxes

Farmers had to pay taxes, too. Tax officials working for the pharaoh measured out the land the farmers had given to each crop, at the start of the year. They figured out how much tax was owed, whether or not the crops succeeded. Tax was paid as a share of what was produced, and if farmers couldn't pay, or didn't want to, they had to go to work on the pyramid instead.

A Shallow Grave

Unlike rich and important people, at the end of a farmer's life there was no fancy tomb. Farmers were buried in shallow, sandy graves. The heat dried out the bodies so that they were preserved.

In this wall painting, farmers harvest grain by hand, in the heat of the sun.

Treats

Some of the tasty foods farmers grew in the warm climate included melons, dates, pomegranates, and figs. They caught fish from the river, too. Although they had a hard life, their diet wasn't too bad.

Busy Housewife

Women were treated with respect in ancient Egypt. They could hold high office and own businesses. However, most of them didn't. Instead they worked on the land, raised a family, and did endless household jobs.

The woman in this ancient relief would have had many jobs to do as a housewife.

Daily Bread

Housewives had to make bread—every day. First, they pounded the grain, then ground it into flour. They added water, shaped the dough into loaves, and baked it in an oven made of mud bricks. They used dried cow dung for fuel. Housewives also made the family's usual drink, beer. This was made from fermented barley bread. Dates and honey were added to make it sweeter. All of this was done while also looking after the children, washing, cleaning, and cooking. It was a busy day!

A Basic Home

An ancient Egyptian house was small and basic. The floor consisted of beaten earth, and there were only a few pieces of furniture, such as stools and mud brick benches. The women would weave rush mats to cover the floor to make it more comfortable. It was a tough job.

The household diet included fish, bread, fruit, and, occasionally, meat from birds.

Terrible Teeth

The ancient Egyptians had terrible teeth, because their bread was full of sand. It blew everywhere, and got into everything, even the bread dough. Over the years, it wore their teeth down to miserable stumps. At least it was the same for both the rich and poor!

Canal Diggers

The flooding of the Nile was the most important event of the year. It was essential to make the most of the life-giving water. It was the horrible job of the canal diggers to make sure the irrigation channels were working at their best.

Dig, Dig, Dig

Canal diggers were outside all day long, digging. They had to dig the huge basins beside the river that collected the floodwater, so it didn't drain away. From these basins they dug a network of irrigation canals that carried the water to the fields, to water the crops. It was backbreaking work, and very wet.

This temple was built for the god Khnum, the ram-headed creator god who caused the Nile flood each year.

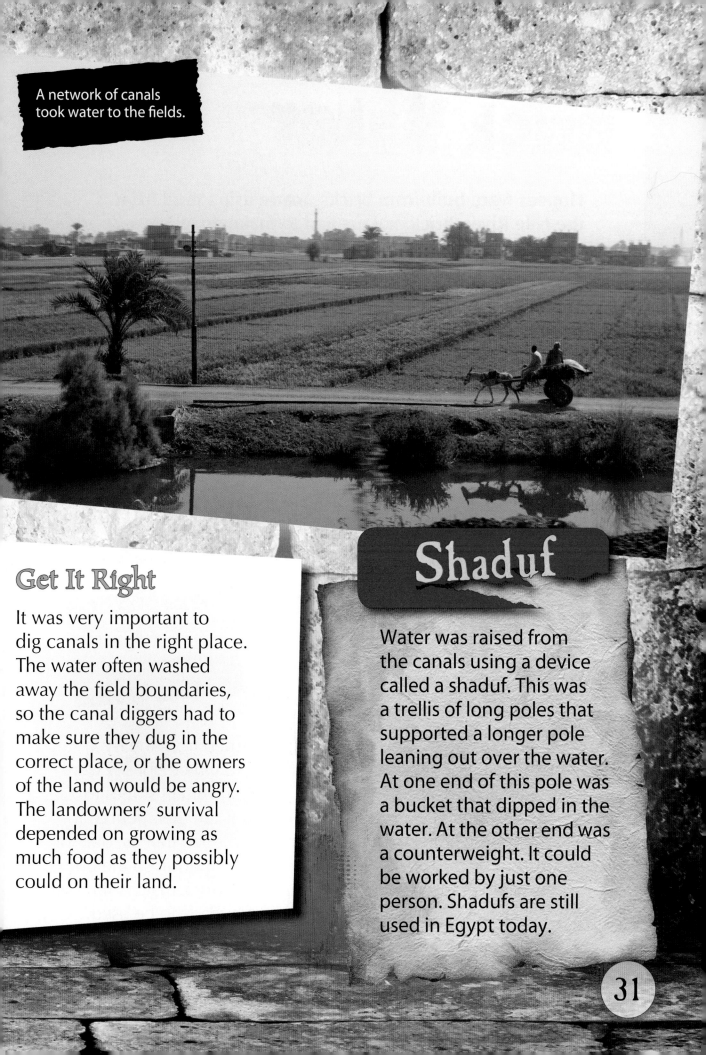

A network of canals took water to the fields.

Get It Right

It was very important to dig canals in the right place. The water often washed away the field boundaries, so the canal diggers had to make sure they dug in the correct place, or the owners of the land would be angry. The landowners' survival depended on growing as much food as they possibly could on their land.

Shaduf

Water was raised from the canals using a device called a shaduf. This was a trellis of long poles that supported a longer pole leaning out over the water. At one end of this pole was a bucket that dipped in the water. At the other end was a counterweight. It could be worked by just one person. Shadufs are still used in Egypt today.

Brick Maker

Houses were built from bricks, made using mud from the Nile River. Brick makers had to make dozens of bricks every day. It was a pretty messy job.

This clay model of a house was put in a person's tomb for use in the afterlife.

Brick makers had to carry pails of heavy mud from the banks of the Nile River.

A Dirty Job

First the brick makers had to gather mud from the river, in leather buckets, and haul it back to where houses were being built. Next, they added straw and small stones to make the mud stronger. They mixed it up, then poured it out into molds. These were simple wooden frames, one for each brick. The frames were left out in the sun so the bricks would dry. When they were hard, the brick makers removed them from the frames, and they were ready to be used.

Comfort for Some

The wealthy had large houses, with many rooms. The windows were always small, though, to keep the house cool. The mud brick walls were plastered and painted with decorations. Up on the roof, foods were laid out to dry in the sun. The wealthy liked to entertain their friends with lavish feasts.

Still Standing

The dry heat of Egypt has preserved some mud brick structures from ancient times. Parts of the walls of the small houses in the village built for pyramid workers at Deir El Medina can still be seen today.

This village at Deir El Medina was built for the workers on the nearby pyramids. They lived away from their own homes for the building season.

Reed Cutter

All along the banks of the Nile grew the tall papyrus plant. This had so many uses in ancient Egypt, but harvesting it was miserable work and could even be fatal.

A Nasty Surprise

Papyrus grows in huge clumps, up to 16 feet (4.8 m) tall. The triangular stems are thick, and topped with a cluster of long, bushy leaves. The reed cutters had to wade through the water, cut through the thick papyrus clumps, and drag them to the bank. They had to be very careful—nearby were hundreds of crocodiles, just waiting for a tasty meal. Reed cutters had to be quick, and keep their wits about them.

Papyrus grows all along the banks of the Nile.

Strips of the papyrus plant were soaked and pressed together, to make a surface that could be used like paper.

A Useful Plant

Young papyrus shoots were cooked and eaten. The roots were made into bowls and other utensils. The thick stems of the plant were the most useful. They were sliced thinly, laid together, and pressed flat to make papyrus paper, for writing on. They were also bound together to make boats, for sailing on the Nile, and woven to make mats, baskets, sandals, and rope. Papyrus paper was light and did not tear easily. It could be rolled into scrolls or cut into sheets. The oldest surviving papyrus roll dates from the twelfth century BC. It is almost 145 feet (44 m) long.

Barber and Wig Maker

The ancient Egyptians loved to look good. They spent lots of time on their hygiene and beauty routines. Barbers and wig makers were well respected, but their jobs were pretty disgusting.

Lousy Louses

The barber's trade began in ancient Egypt. Both men and women shaved their heads, to get rid of nits and lice. That was the horrible job of the barber. They even had to shave the entire bodies of some high ranking officials! They cleaned their ears and checked their teeth. It was an up-close and personal job.

Men shaved their heads and then wore short wigs.

Sweet-Smelling Fat

If you were going out for a special occasion, it was essential to smell sweet. The barber gave you a cone of fat to stick on top of your wig. It was scented with perfumes, and in the heat of the evening it slowly melted down your head. Lovely!

Waxy Wigs

Having shaved off their hair, many people wore a wig. The poor wig maker used beeswax to stick together pieces of wool or vegetable fibers. For the rich, the wig makers used human hair. Women's wigs were long and thick, men's were shorter but more complex. The more important the person, the more elaborate their wig would be.

This tomb carving shows a beautiful woman with an elaborate wig.

Coffin Maker

The afterlife was such an important part of the culture of ancient Egypt that it was essential to have a suitable coffin for the journey ahead.

The insides of coffins were painted with scenes to help the dead person on their journey to the afterlife.

Early Styles

Coffins from early Egyptian times were simple wooden boxes. Even these had to be prepared correctly. Spells were painted all over the insides, to help the person on their scary journey to the afterlife. Sometimes a map of the underworld was painted on the coffin, to help the deceased find his or her way. If the coffin maker didn't get the painting right the poor dead person would have a terrible afterlife! More spells and a pair of eyes were painted on the outside of the coffin, so the dead person could see, and a pair of false doors, so they could get out.

Human Shape

From about 1950 BC, coffins changed shape. Now the job of coffin makers became more difficult as coffins were created in the shape of human bodies. For some important people there were several coffins, one inside the other. Coffin makers from different cities developed their own individual styles.

Hieroglyphs

Spells on the coffins were written in hieroglyphs. This was the Egyptians' form of picture writing, and it was complicated. It included about 700 different signs, and might be read either from right to left, left to right, or top to bottom.

There are hieroglyphs painted on the yellow bands around this human-shaped coffin.

Chapter Four
Away from Home

Ancient Egypt was not isolated. The pharaohs loved to trade with their neighbors. The Egyptians traveled to the countries surrounding them to both sell and buy goods. The Egyptians also protected themselves from any neighbors that might try to invade their country. Egyptian armies were made up of soldiers whose job it was to fight, and if necessary die, for the glory of their god-king.

Traders brought back goods from Africa, such as spices and animal skins.

Trade

Some of the riches of Egypt, such as its gold, were traded with countries such as Syria to the north and Nubia to the south. Merchants had the dangerous job of traveling to these places, and up the Nile to unknown countries in Africa. From there they brought back elephant tusks, giraffe tails, panther skins, and live animals such as lions.

A Life of Service

For soldiers, life away from home was extremely challenging. They fought hard, in campaigns in Palestine, Syria, and Nubia. The pharaoh was, of course, head of the army. A foot soldier was armed with a wooden shield, spear, and a battle axe. Charioteers plunged into battle on horse-drawn chariots. They carried a group of archers, shooting arrows. The training was very hard, discipline was strict, and if soldiers stepped out of line the punishments were very severe.

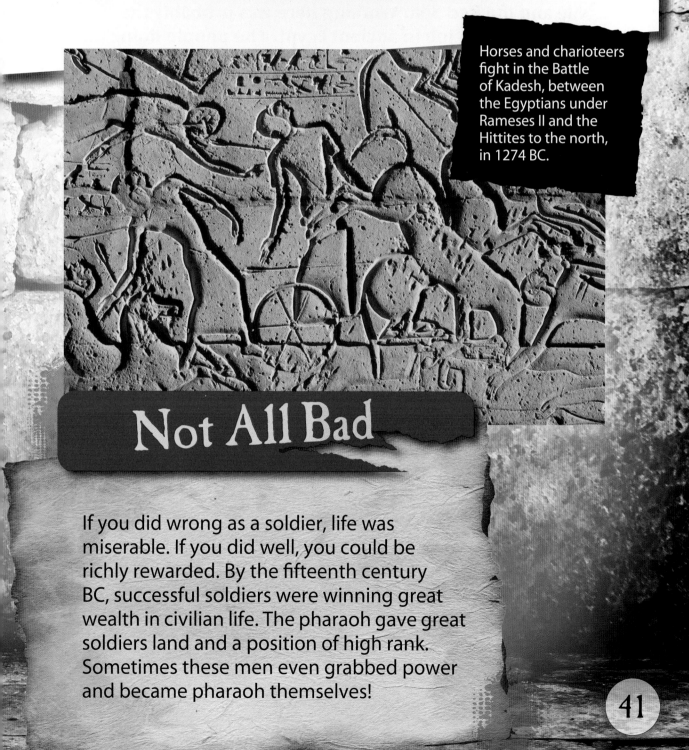

Horses and charioteers fight in the Battle of Kadesh, between the Egyptians under Rameses II and the Hittites to the north, in 1274 BC.

Not All Bad

If you did wrong as a soldier, life was miserable. If you did well, you could be richly rewarded. By the fifteenth century BC, successful soldiers were winning great wealth in civilian life. The pharaoh gave great soldiers land and a position of high rank. Sometimes these men even grabbed power and became pharaoh themselves!

Miserable Mining

The Egyptians loved gold, which they believed had special properties. They used it to make lavish jewelry, and to adorn the coffins of the pharaohs. The gold came mostly from mines in Nubia, to the south between the Nile and the Red Sea. Working here was probably the most miserable job in ancient Egypt. The people doing this horrible job were usually criminals and slaves.

Hard Grind

The specks of gold were embedded in hard rock, deep underground. The rock was blasted away by heating it up with fires, then throwing cold water on it to make it shatter. Miners were down in the smoky darkness doing this, day after day. They hauled blocks of rock to the surface where others crushed them until they were piles of dust.

The lavish burial mask of the pharaoh Tutankhamun is one of the most famous gold objects from ancient Egypt.

Extracting the Gold

The gold was extracted from the powdered rock using water. A stream of water washed over it, carrying away all materials except the gold, which was the heaviest. Even women, children, and old men were put to this awful labor. The overseer cracked his whip to keep everyone working.

This carving from the tomb of Rameses III shows the goddess Nephthys seated on the Egyptian hieroglyph for "gold."

Godly Gold

The Egyptian word for gold was *nub*. This is how Nubia got its name. Gold was thought to be the skin of the gods. Only the pharaoh and the highest officials were permitted to wear gold jewelry. Small gold statues of the gods were used for religious ceremonies.

The End of the Pharaohs

During the last 1,000 years BC, foreigners began to invade Egypt. First the Persians, then the Greeks swept in. But the decline of ancient Egypt took a long time, and the horrible jobs certainly did not come to a sudden stop.

Labor Goes On

One of the latest pharaohs was also one of the greatest. Rameses II ruled in the thirteenth century BC for an amazing 67 years. He built so many temples, statues, and monuments that there were more than enough horrible building jobs to be done. One of the greatest was the temple that Rameses had cut into the rock at Abu Simbel, near Thebes. Four vast statues of Rameses guarded the façade, built by hundreds of workers. He made them carve his features extra deeply, so that they would survive for longer.

These colossal statues of Rameses II stand at the entrance to his rock temple at Abu Simbel. He built two temples there as lasting monuments to himself and his queen, Nefertari.

Laborers toiled over another huge temple complex, at Luxor. This had been started by earlier pharaohs. Rameses added more to it, including two huge obelisks that had to be hauled into place outside the new ceremonial gateway. Rameses' successors worked their soldiers hard, defending the country against raiders and invaders. Finally, in 30 BC, Egypt passed into the control of the Romans.

Rameses II had this massive obelisk built for his temple at Luxor.

Tomb of Nefertari

Nefertari was a wife of Rameses II. Her lavishly decorated tomb is one of the wonders of ancient Egyptian art. It shows the incredible skills of the many people who built and decorated it. Their jobs may sometimes have been horrible, but their work was wonderful.

Glossary

afterlife life after death

amulet a magical charm worn to protect people from harm

architects people who design buildings

bartered traded services or things without using money

canopic jar a special jar used to store the intestines, liver, lungs, and stomach of dead people for the afterlife

civilization the culture of a particular society that has reached an advanced level

counterweight a weight that exactly balances another weight

embedded to set firmly in a surrounding material

fertile to be able to produce farm crops or other plant life

flourished grew in a strong, healthy way

government a group of people who give direction and have control in a place

governors people who lead a government

hieroglyphs the Egyptian form of picture writing

irrigation the supply of water to land by man-made means

lice small insects that live on people's or animals' hair or skin

merchants people who buy and sell goods for profit

natron a type of salt, used in laundry and in embalming dead bodies

nits the eggs of lice

obelisks tall, thin stone columns with tapering sides rising to a point

officials people who hold office in a government

overseer a person in charge of laborers

papyrus a tall, reedlike plant that grew along the Nile, used for making paper, boats, and other objects

parasites plants, animals, or fungi that live on or in another living thing

pharaoh a ruler of ancient Egypt

preserved kept from rotting

prosperity a state of being wealthy and successful

province the parts of a country outside its main cities

resin a sticky substance found inside trees

sarcophagus a stone coffin that held the inner coffins

shabtis small statues of workers, placed in a person's tomb to look after them in the afterlife

shaduf a device for raising water from the Nile, using a weight and a bucket

spirits forces that are thought to be part of a human being

starch a substance used to make clothing stiff

For More Information

Books

Boyer, Crispin. *National Geographic Kids Everything Ancient Egypt.* Washington, DC: National Geographic, 2011.

Sheldon, Ken, ed. *If I Were a Kid in Ancient Egypt.* Peterborough, NH: Cricket Books, 2006.

Hart, George. *Ancient Egypt.* New York, NY: DK Publishing, 2004.

Websites

Check out this fun website to see how the Egyptians built the pyramids. You can also find out all about the Nile River, the Egyptian Empire, and how Egypt declined:
www.kidspast.com/world-history/0032-egyptian-pyramids.php

Find out some fast facts about Egyptian life at this web page:
www.kidskonnect.com/subjectindex/16-educational/history/253-ancient-egypt.html

Find out about the pharaohs, queens, hieroglyphics and much more at this website:
www.ducksters.com/history/ancient_egypt.php

Publisher's note to educators and parents: Our editors have carefully reviewed these websites to ensure that they are suitable for students. Many websites change frequently, however, and we cannot guarantee that a site's future contents will continue to meet our high standards of quality and educational value. Be advised that students should be closely supervised whenever they access the Internet.

Index

Abu Simbel 44
afterlife 5, 9, 12, 13, 15, 22, 32, 38
Amun-Ra 14

barbers 7, 36–37
bread 28, 29

canopic jars 12
coffins 5, 13, 17, 38–39, 42

Djoser 14

embalming 12–13

farming 5, 26–27

Giza 14, 16
gods 7, 14, 15, 24, 25, 30, 43
gold 40, 42–43

Hatshepsut 7, 15
hieroglyphs 39
houses 28, 32–33

irrigation 30–31

Karnak 23
Khufu 14

laundry 10–11
leisure 24
Luxor 4, 45

Merneith, Queen 8–9
mining 42–43
mummies 11, 12, 13

natron 11, 13
Nefertari, Queen 45
Nile River 5, 11, 15, 16, 18, 24, 26,
   30, 32, 34, 35, 40, 42
Nubia 40, 41, 42, 43

obelisks 17, 45
officials 4, 27, 36, 43

Palestine 41
papyrus 34–35
Persians 44
pharaohs 4, 6–7, 10, 11, 12, 14, 15,
   19, 22, 23, 25, 27, 40, 41, 42, 43,
   44–45
priests 4
pyramids 14–23, 27, 33

quarrying 16–17, 18

Rameses II 41, 44, 45
religion 25
Romans 45

sarcophagus 17
slaves 4, 42
soldiers 40, 41, 45
Syria 40, 41

taxation 6, 18, 27
temples 4, 5, 7, 15, 23, 25, 30, 44,
   45
tombs 5, 9, 12, 14, 15, 17, 22, 25,
   27, 32, 37, 43, 45
trade 5, 7, 36, 40

wigs 7, 36–37
women 28, 36, 37, 43